Rena Kuhl

First published in Great Britain in 1983 by
Hodder and Stoughton Children's Books

This edition published in 1989 by
Treasure Press
Michelin House
81 Fulham Road
London SW3 6RB

Text copyright © 1983 Keith Faulkner
Illustrations copyright © 1983 Keith Faulkner

ISBN 1 85051 353 8

Produced by Mandarin Offset
Printed and bound in Hong Kong

*First Questions*
about

# TRANSPORT

## Keith Faulkner

TREASURE PRESS

Produced by Keith Faulkner Publishing Limited

Advisor: Bill Gunston

Illustrated by:

Dick Eastland
Philip Emms
Wilf Hardy
Richard Hook
Jonathan Lambert
Mike Roffe
Temple Art Agency
Trevor White

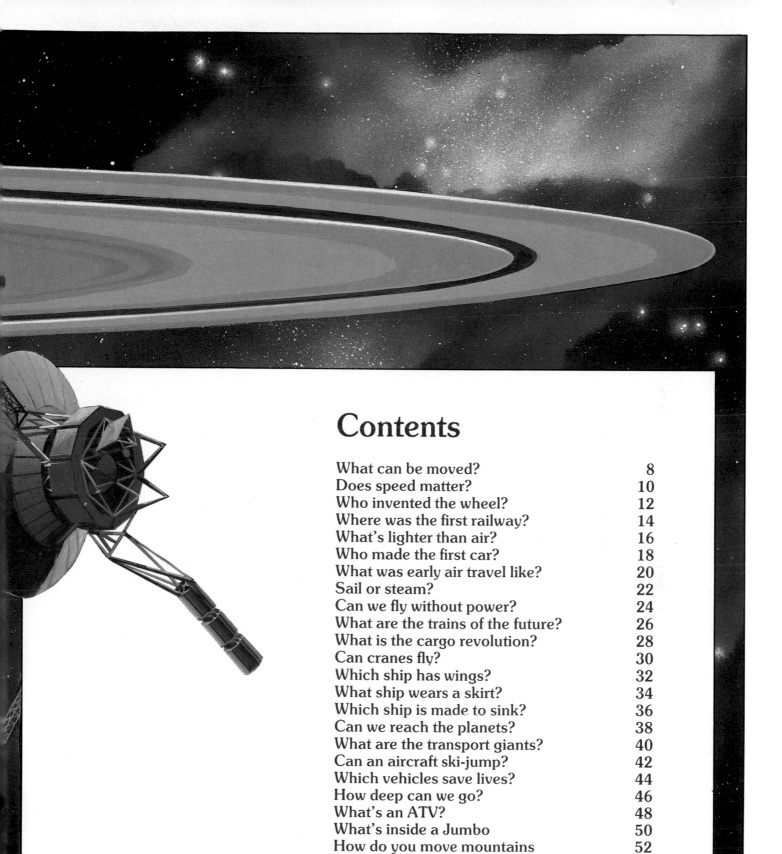

# Contents

# What can be moved?

Early man had only his own strength with which to move heavy objects. With the invention of wheels, pulleys and levers, this strength was greatly increased. In 200 B.C. the ancient Greek scientist Archimedes built a pulley system that enabled one man to haul a ship onto the shore. The Pyramids of Egypt and Central America, and the Great Wall of China, were built with materials moved using only simple machines of this kind. In some places, single blocks of stone weighing more than 40 tonnes were transported using no more than wooden rollers, ropes and the muscle power of thousands of slaves.

Even these great feats of building from the past cannot match our ability today. With the help of modern technology, almost anything can be moved.

This huge buoy is the heaviest load ever moved on wheels. A 1,024 wheeled transporter carried its weight of 3,200 tonnes.

This vast church, built in Czechoslovakia in 1518, was in the way of a coalmine. It was saved by moving it 841m on a specially built railway. The church was supported in a steel frame for the journey, which was completed after 8yrs of preparation.

The world's largest single vehicle carried the Saturn V rockets to the launch site. As the rockets were 111m tall and weighed 2850 tonnes and the crawler itself weighs 5000 tonnes, the total combined weight was over 8000 tonnes.

# Does speed matter?

In these days of high-speed cars, trains and supersonic aircraft, it is difficult to imagine a time when the horse was the fastest means of transport. A horse can run further and faster than a man, and can carry a heavier load. Probably the horse was an even more important stage of transport than the motorcar, which has only been around for a hundred years.

Transport efficiency can be measured in several ways – speed, economy and capacity. Every kind of transport system has different requirements. Mail and people in a hurry travel by high-speed aircraft, but bulk cargoes, such as grain or oil, are carried in relatively slow cargo ships.

A single horse can haul this heavy barge on the canal. The same load on wagons might need four or even five horses to pull it.

Speeds have increased at an amazing rate since early times, the greatest increase being over the past century, due to the internal combustion and jet engines.

Bullock cart 3.21kph

1808

Early steam engine 19.30kph

Steam coach 21.18kph

1827

Early motorcyc[le] 1894 45kph

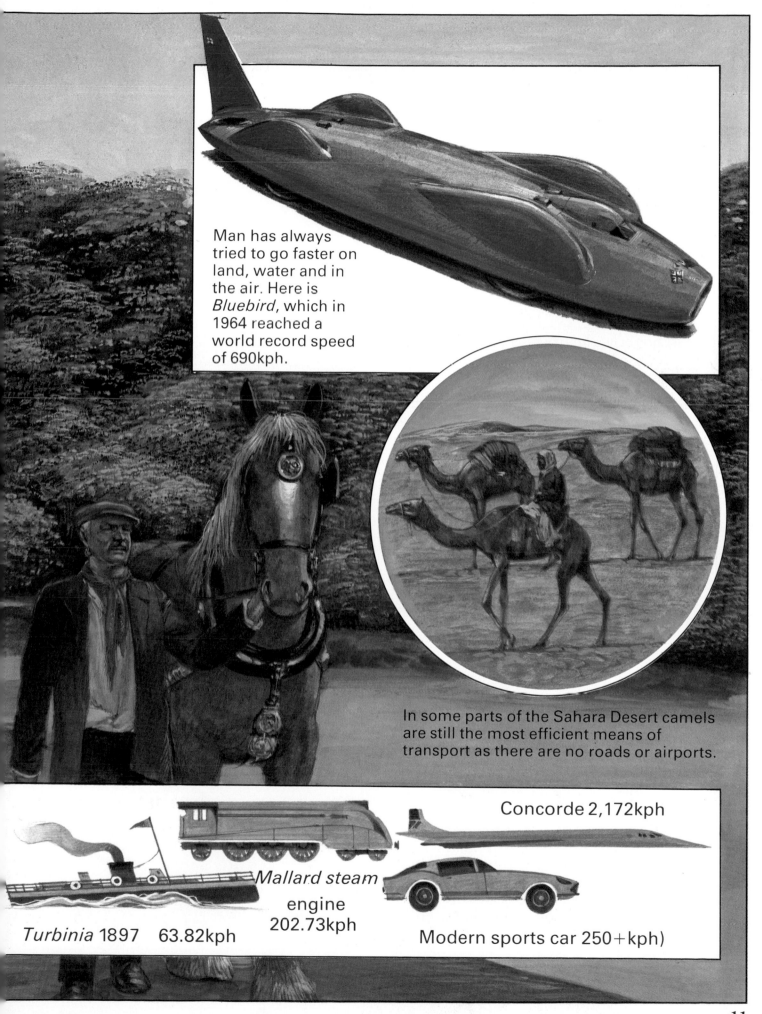

Man has always tried to go faster on land, water and in the air. Here is *Bluebird*, which in 1964 reached a world record speed of 690kph.

In some parts of the Sahara Desert camels are still the most efficient means of transport as there are no roads or airports.

Concorde 2,172kph

*Mallard steam* engine 202.73kph

*Turbinia* 1897    63.82kph

Modern sports car 250+kph)

11

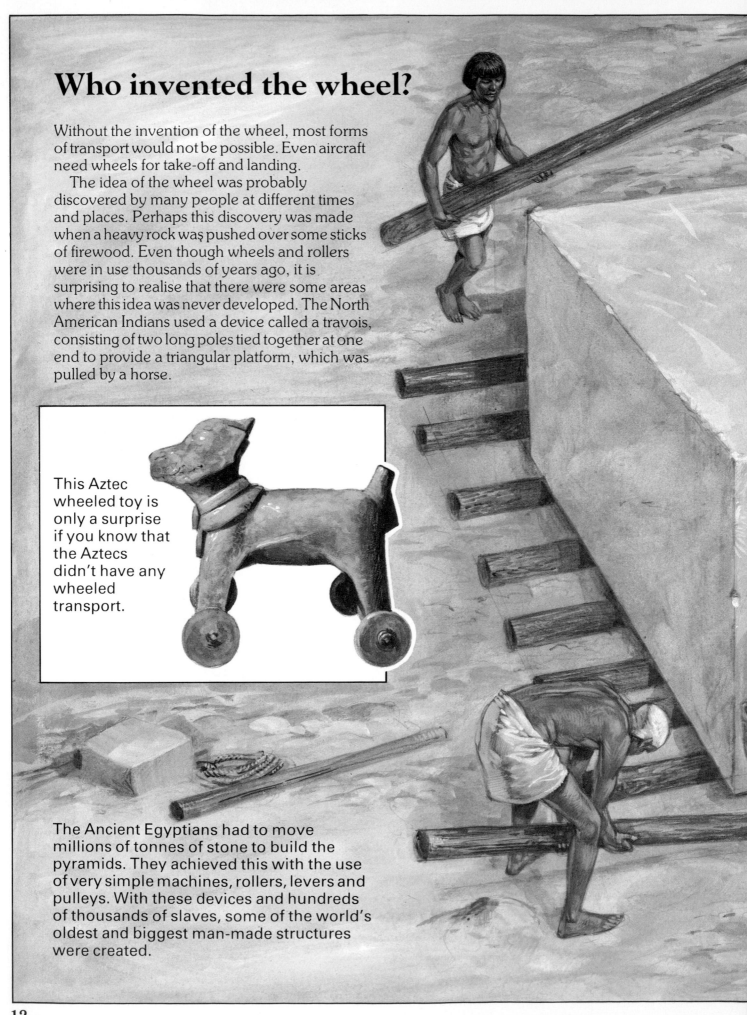

# Who invented the wheel?

Without the invention of the wheel, most forms of transport would not be possible. Even aircraft need wheels for take-off and landing.

The idea of the wheel was probably discovered by many people at different times and places. Perhaps this discovery was made when a heavy rock was pushed over some sticks of firewood. Even though wheels and rollers were in use thousands of years ago, it is surprising to realise that there were some areas where this idea was never developed. The North American Indians used a device called a travois, consisting of two long poles tied together at one end to provide a triangular platform, which was pulled by a horse.

This Aztec wheeled toy is only a surprise if you know that the Aztecs didn't have any wheeled transport.

The Ancient Egyptians had to move millions of tonnes of stone to build the pyramids. They achieved this with the use of very simple machines, rollers, levers and pulleys. With these devices and hundreds of thousands of slaves, some of the world's oldest and biggest man-made structures were created.

The history of the wheel goes back many thousands of years. From the log rollers of prehistoric man, to the light chariot wheels of Ancient Egypt and Assyria, and then through time to the modern rubber-tyred wheels of today.

# Where was the first railway?

In the days before smooth roads, the cart tracks were rough and rutted from the heavy wagon wheels. This limited the load that a horse could pull, until a smoother surface could be provided. The first rail-ways did just this, by giving each wheel a smooth, but narrow, road to run on, the only problem being to keep the wheels on the narrow track.

The first tracks were wood or stone slabs, with a ridge or flange on the outside to guide the wheels. It was the combination of metal track and the steam engine which led to the beginnings of the railway, as we now know it. With Richard Trevithick's steam engine *Pen-y-darren* in 1804, the age of railways had begun.

An early horse-drawn railway. In places where the wagon had to be hauled up a slope to be emptied, the driver and the horse could both ride in the empty wagon back to the bottom again.

In 1811, Blenkinsop built his locomotive with cog-like driving wheels which gripped onto pegs on the sides of the rails.

After the days of wood or stone tracks, cast iron was the obvious material for building rails. At the beginning, the rails were flanged to guide the wheels, but a little later the flanged wheel appeared. The wheels and rails were later made of steel.

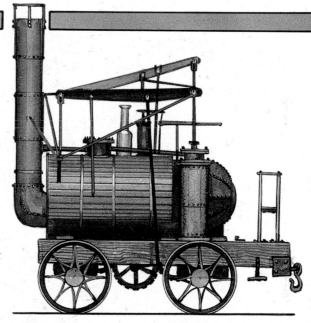

*Puffing Billy* was built in 1813 by W. Hedley, who closely followed the work of Blenkinsop. The engine drove all four wheels and so had a better grip on the rails, without Blenkinsop's system.

The *Rocket*, built by Robert and George Stephenson, is probably the best known early locomotive. It won the Rainhill Trials, a competition between several engines in 1829. The *Rocket* hauled a load of 3 tonnes and achieved a top speed of 38.6kph.

# What's lighter than air?

Balloons provided man with his first experience of flight after centuries of dreaming. On November 21 1783, the world's first aerial voyage took place in Paris.

Many years before this, others had thought of the idea. In 1670, Francesco de Lana had designed a flying ship supported by large, hollow copper balls, from which the air has been removed. Although this was not successful, he accurately predicted the use of aircraft in warfare, for both bombing and transport.

The Montgolfier brothers discovered that hot air could provide the lifting power, as it is lighter than cold air, and only ten days later J.A.C. Charles ascended in the first hydrogen-filled balloon. The age of aircraft had begun.

The LZ127 *Graf Zeppelin* launched in 1928 was as big as many ocean liners. It was 236m long and equipped with comfortable cabins and lounges for its passengers. Until World War II it dominated the skies, travelling to every part of the globe. The LZ130 shown here was planned but not built.

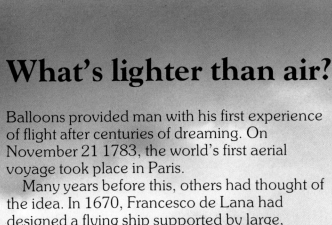

History was made on 21 November 1783 by Pilâtre de Rozier and the Marquis d'Arlandes in the Montgolfier hot-air balloon, the world's first manned flight.

Fin

Elevator

Rudder

Landing wheel

Girder framework

D-LZ130

Engine car

Oil tanks

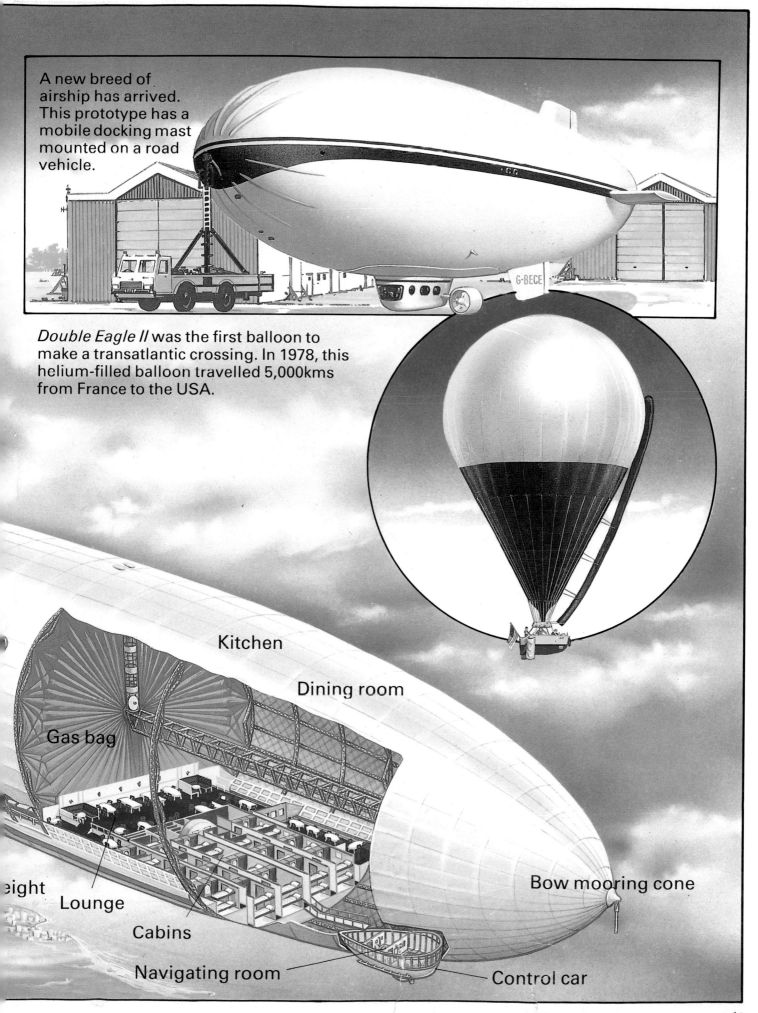

A new breed of airship has arrived. This prototype has a mobile docking mast mounted on a road vehicle.

*Double Eagle II* was the first balloon to make a transatlantic crossing. In 1978, this helium-filled balloon travelled 5,000kms from France to the USA.

Gas bag

Kitchen

Dining room

eight

Lounge

Cabins

Navigating room

Bow mooring cone

Control car

# Who made the first car?

The idea of the horseless carriage began in 1705 with the development of the steam engine. The real beginning of the motorcar had to wait a less cumbersome form of power, the internal-combustion engine.

At the beginning of the 19th century, the first of these new engines started to appear, but it was not until 80 years later that the first real motorcar took to the road.

Siegfried Marcus, an Austrian inventor and engineer, is credited by some people as the original inventor of the motorcar. In 1865 he designed and built an internal-combustion engine and fitted it to a four-wheeled handcart.

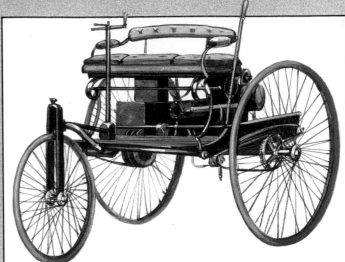

The first real motorcar was built by Karl Benz in 1885. It had a water-cooled engine.

The 1988 Daimler was one of the first recognisable cars arranged as many cars still are. It had rubber-tyred wheels, headlamps, and an enclosed front engine with rear wheel drive.

Henry Ford did not invent motorcars, but he was the first to build them in great numbers. The Ford Motor Company started in 1903, and in 1908 produced its famous Model T which sold over 15 million.

In 1769 Nicholas Cugnot built this steam carriage. Though not a motorcar, it was possibly the world's first self-propelled vehicle.

This 1903 Curved Dash Oldsmobile was the best selling car in the United States before Henry Ford built the Model T. It had a top speed of 32kph.

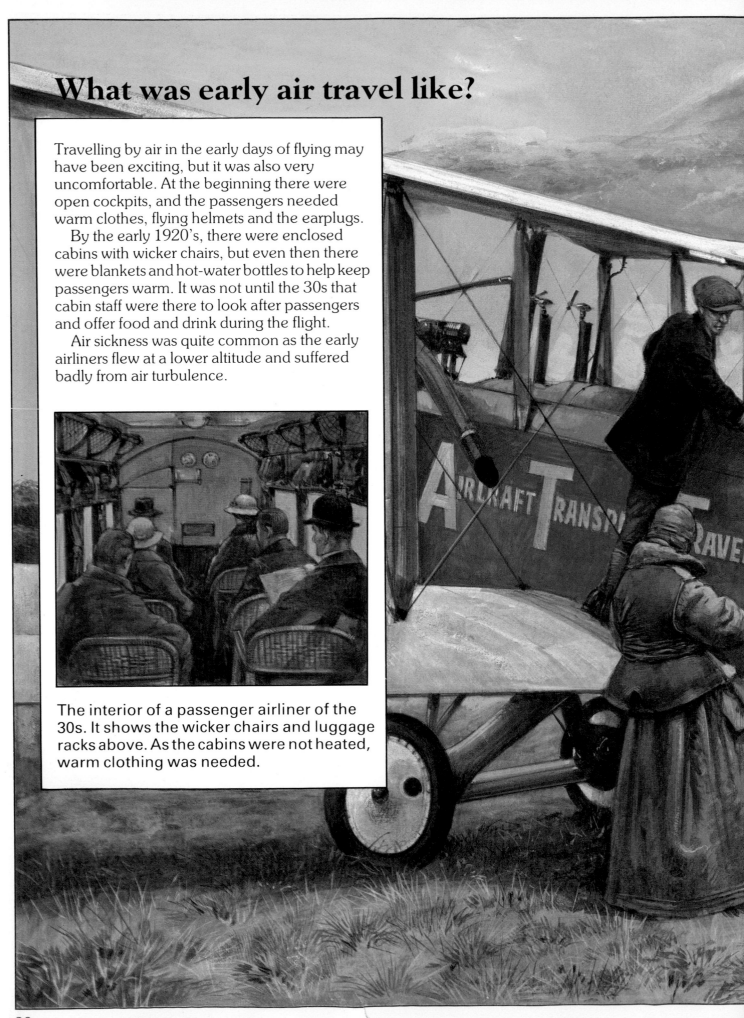

# What was early air travel like?

Travelling by air in the early days of flying may have been exciting, but it was also very uncomfortable. At the beginning there were open cockpits, and the passengers needed warm clothes, flying helmets and the earplugs.

By the early 1920's, there were enclosed cabins with wicker chairs, but even then there were blankets and hot-water bottles to help keep passengers warm. It was not until the 30s that cabin staff were there to look after passengers and offer food and drink during the flight.

Air sickness was quite common as the early airliners flew at a lower altitude and suffered badly from air turbulence.

The interior of a passenger airliner of the 30s. It shows the wicker chairs and luggage racks above. As the cabins were not heated, warm clothing was needed.

Air travel in the era of open-cockpit bi-planes was a cold and bumpy ordeal. But there were plenty of people eager to try this exciting new form of transport.

Pullman 1918

HP42 1930

DC9 1965

Jumbo 1968

The standard of comfort has changed in sixty years, from the wicker chairs of the 20s to the air-conditioned luxury of today's Jumbo Jet.

# Sail or steam?

The development of steam power had a great effect on all forms of transport. The first self-propelled vehicles on both road and rail were steam-driven. The first steam-powered boat was built in France in 1776. It was the first of many, and gradually the great sailing ships which had ruled the oceans began to disappear.

When the first reliable steamships were built, they offered great advantages over sailing vessels. In the early days they were not faster, but they could not be becalmed or driven far off their course by the wind.

Throughout the 19th century more steamships were built, and by 1900 the era of the sailing ship was over, although a few remain in service even today, for training purposes.

*Cutty Sark*, one of the last great sailing ships, was built in 1869. In 1957 she was saved from destruction, rebuilt, and is now near the Maritime Museum in Greenwich, London.

This Japanese experimental ship, the *Aitokumaru*, has computer-controlled rigid 'sails' to use windpower, in addition to conventional engines.

The *Great Eastern* steamship was built by Sir Isambard Brunel and completed in 1858. Built of iron, she was 210.9m long and weighed 18,626 tonnes. The *Great Eastern's* first Atlantic crossing was in June 1860, carrying 4,000 passengers at an average speed of 14 knots.

The argument was not only between sail and steam, but also between screw (propeller) and paddlewheel. In 1845, a tug-of-war was held between the steam sloops *Rattler* (screw) and *Alecto* (paddle). The screw-driven *Rattler* won easily, pulling *Alecto* backwards at almost 3 knots.

# Can we fly without power?

Since the earliest times, man has longed to fly like the birds. Almost 500 years ago, Leonardo da Vinci was designing man-powered flying machines, but it has taken all this time to achieve success.

The problem is that, compared with birds, we have small muscles and a heavy body. It was not until recently that the combination of ultra-light materials and computer-aided design led to one of the first really successful man-powered flights. As this success was due to a wing span of 28.35m, and a racing cyclist as pilot, it seems unlikely that man-powered flight could ever be a means of transport for everyday use.

Although not the first man-powered aircraft to fly, the *Gossamer Albatross*, shown below, made the first real journey. On 12 June 1979, it made a successful channel crossing from Dover to Calais in 2 hours 49 mins. A Californian racing cyclist, Bryan Allen, was both the pilot and the 'engine' for this historic flight.

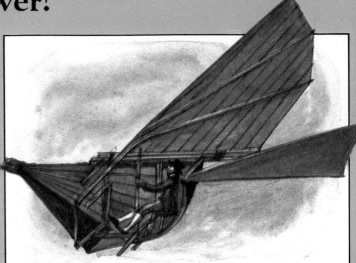

Many of man's early attempts at designing flying machines were directly copied from birds. In this example, the designer has fitted his machine with a bird's head, complete with beak.

Modern gliders or sailplanes may not be man-powered, but they are a way of flying without power. Most gliders are launched by being towed by a light aircraft.

The *Hatfield Puffin* was an early, but limited, success. In 1962 it flew a distance of 908m. The name *Puffin* was chosen because it took a lot of 'puffing' to fly it.

The hang glider was developed in the early 60s and is now the cheapest and most common form of private sport flying.

# What are the trains of the future?

Pictures of imaginary cities of the future often show gleaming high-speed trains, streaking through the futuristic landscape. Indeed, the railway has much to offer as a means of transport to suit very different needs.

As early as 1955, high-speed trains were reaching speeds of 331kph in France, but these were experimental and the speed could not be maintained in a regular service. The high-speed train of the future could easily compete with aircraft on an overland journey. In Japan, in 1979, an experimental train travelled at a speed of 504kph.

Another area being developed is that of city rail transport. In this situation, trains compete with cars. A small computer train full of passengers is far more economical, and takes up much less space, than the same number of people travelling in separate motorcars.

The HSST (High-Speed Surface Transport) is a Maglev, short for magnetic levitation. The train has no wheels, and is held up by magnetism.

The TGV of the French railways is powered by gas-turbine engines. It is capable of sustaining speeds of almost 300kph.

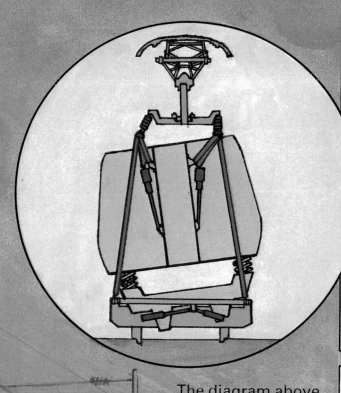

British Rail's APT (Advanced Passenger Train) has a special tilting mechanism. This is to minimise discomfort when travelling round a bend at speeds over 200kph.

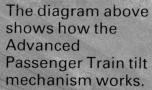

The diagram above shows how the Advanced Passenger Train tilt mechanism works.

Overhead monorails have many advantages for rapid city transport. Through easily accessible for passengers, they leave the city streets clear for pedestrians.

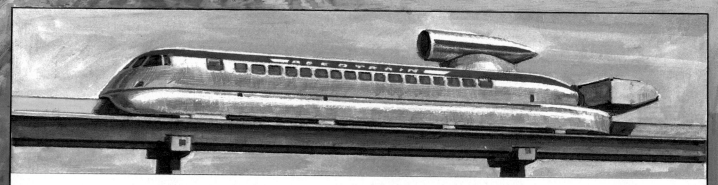

Not all experimental trains are a success. This French hover-train project was abandoned, even though it reached a speed of 426kph. Perhaps in the future the problems can be solved and high-speed hover-trains will then become a possibility.

# What is the cargo revolution?

Ships have been used to transport goods for thousands of years. Not only the ships themselves have changed dramatically since the days of the Roman galleys, but also the methods of loading and unloading the goods.

Early quays and dockyards employed large numbers of people, the goods were either carried down the gangplanks or slung from simple cranes in nets or baskets.

The use of containers is a relatively recent development. It not only saves time and manpower, but greatly reduces the proportion of goods damaged or stolen. The container system is very simple: each container is a standard size unit which will stack together and fit a wide range of different transport systems.

This giant crane can move along the dockside on rails. It lifts the containers and can place them straight on to a waiting truck or train. It can also stack them on the dockside, and as they are weatherproof they do not need warehouses.

Standard containers will fit aircraft, ships, trucks and trains. In special container docks a crane can lift the container from the ship, straight on to a truck or train.

Bulk cargoes, like grain, are not suitable for containers. Grain is now unloaded by vast suction tubes.

Bulk cargoes were originally unloaded manually – grain in sacks, and liquids in barrels and casks.

# Can cranes fly?

Leonardo da Vinci made drawings of helicopters in the 15th century, but it was not until 1936 that the first helicopter flew. Louis Bregeut was the first man to leave the ground in a rotating wing aircraft, for a sustained flight.

The helicopter industry was started by Igor Sikorsky, in the USA. His VS300 helicopter flew in 1939 and was the forerunner of the modern helicopter. Helicopters are very versatile machines, and perform many useful tasks. Their main advantage is the small landing area they require, which makes them ideal for city transport, warfare and rescue work. The helicopter is also used as a flying crane to reach inaccessible places, and carry heavy loads where a conventional crane cannot go.

Since the first flight in 1936, there have been tremendous developments in helicopter design. A tilt-rotor research aircraft attained a speed of 557.8kph in 1980.

This Russian Mil Mi-26 is the world's largest and most powerful helicopter. Here it is seen carrying an electricity pylon over the frozen wastes of Siberia.

A Bell 222 lands on a roof-top heliport in a city centre. The World Trade Centre in New York has a helipad on its roof 422m above the busy streets below.

A Westland Sea King used for air/sea rescue. Thousands of lives have been saved by this method. The winchman lowers the rescuer who has a harness to lift people from the sea, or the deck of a sinking ship.

This Sikorsky CH-53E is carrying a damaged aircraft from an aircraft carrier to a land base for repairs. These helicopters are also used to transport men and equipment to and from the battlefield.

# Which ship has wings?

The speed of a ship is greatly reduced by the drag of water on the ship's hull. The hydrofoil was developed in order to reduce drag by lifting most of the vessel out of the water.

Hydrofoils are, in fact, underwater wings. The water flowing round the aerofoil shape which creates the lift. At slow speeds the boat behaves in the normal way with the hull floating in the water. It is only as the speed increases that the foil produces enough lift for the hull to rise clear of the water.

An American naval hydrofoil, *Plainview*, launched in 1965, is 65m long and weighs 310 tonnes loaded. A typical commercial hydrofoil is the Supramar PTS 150 MkIII, which carries up to 250 passengers at 74kph.

A Boeing Jetfoil carrying its 250 passengers at a cruising speed of 80kph. This hydrofoil does not have propellers, but is driven by high-powered jets of water.

The LVHX2 hydrofoil landing craft is a very stange mixture. On land it is an armoured truck, in the water it floats like a boat, and at high speed it 'flies' through the water on hydrofoils.

Most hydrofoils are of the surface piercing type. The foils are V-shaped. As the ship's speed increases and the hull clears the water, less of the foil is submerged, so that at top speed very little drag is created.

Surface piercing

Deep foil

Shallow foil

Although the hydrofoil is a flying boat, the idea was developed much earlier. In the early days of aviation an aircraft that could take off and land on water was a popular means of transport. Not requiring runways made it especially useful, as few airports had been built. The Dornier Do. X, a giant twelve-engined flying boat, in use during the 30s, was obviously at home on the water, with its boat-like fuselage.

# What ship wears a skirt?

Early in the 1950s Christopher Cockerell, an electrical engineer, had an idea. To test his idea, he used a vacuum cleaner, kitchen scales and two tin cans. It was this test that led to the development of the hovercraft.

Hovercraft or air-cushion vehicles are able to travel faster and use less power than boats because there is no water resistance. They can also travel on land and over swampy ground, making them useful for military and rescue purposes. The flexible skirt seals in the air-cushion to conserve power and allows the vehicle to clear obstacles without damage.

The hovercraft principle has also been applied to other vehicles. Very heavy loads are transported by road using hover-platforms, this spreads the weight and avoids damaging the road surface. Even some heavy transport aircraft have used an air-cushion instead of a wheeled landing gear.

Air-cushion vehicles have many uses. Here, a small air-cushion platform supports the landing gear of a huge air-liner. As there is no friction, two men can easily move the vast aircraft.

The Super 4, weighing 160 tonnes, carries up to 418 passengers and 59 cars at about 100kph on the cross Channel routes from England to France.

Air drawn in by fan

The diagram above shows how a hover-craft works. Air is sucked in at the top and pumped down through the flexible skirt, which directs the air inwards to create the pressure necessary to support the vehicle. The air then escapes through the small gap between the skirt and the water.

The tools of invention used by Christopher Cockerell: a vacuum cleaner motor to blow, not suck, the air; two cans, one inside the other; and kitchen scales to measure the lifting power of the air pressure.

HOVER*SPEED*

# Which ship is made to sink?

In 1962 the US Navy launched a very special ship. It was called FLIP (Floating Instrument Platform) and was very special because, unlike other ships, it was designed to sink. FLIP was built to measure wave patterns and strength, which is important in understanding the weather. It also helps us to design oil rigs and other equipment for exploiting the ocean's natural resources.

There have always been special ships for special purposes, from icebreakers capable of smashing through ice 4m thick, to floating hotels complete with swimming pools and cinemas. Every vessel must not only suit its specific job, but also be able to cope with the extremes of weather at sea.

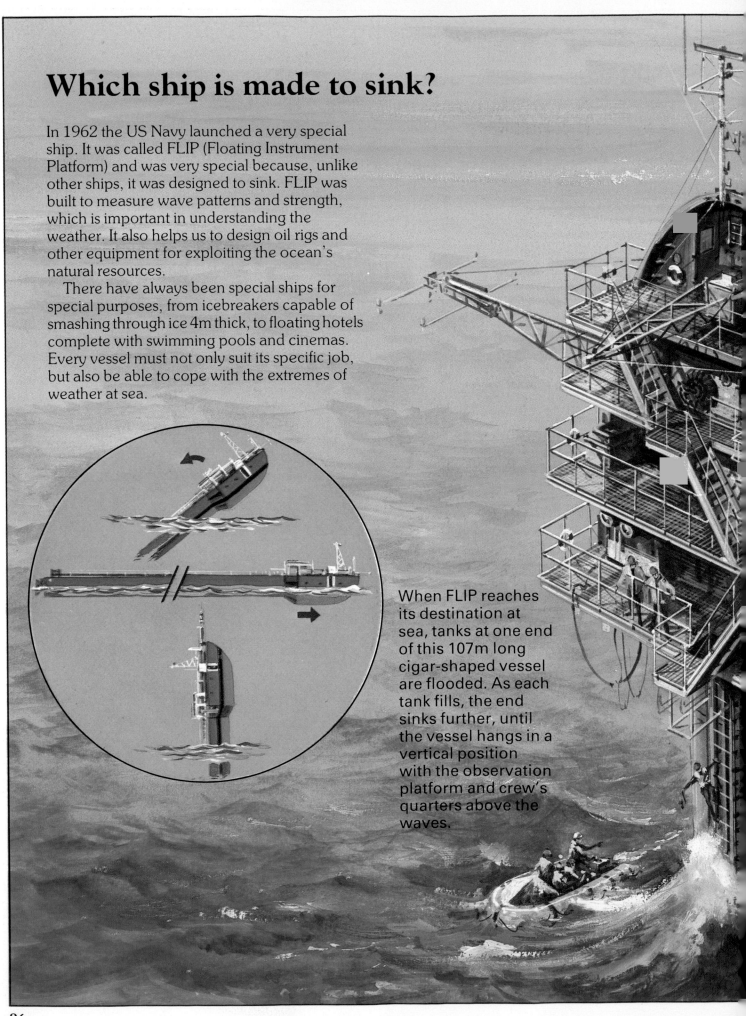

When FLIP reaches its destination at sea, tanks at one end of this 107m long cigar-shaped vessel are flooded. As each tank fills, the end sinks further, until the vessel hangs in a vertical position with the observation platform and crew's quarters above the waves.

SWATH (Small Waterplane Area Twin Hull) is a new type of ship designed to save energy. It floats on two buoyant torpedo-shaped pylons, reducing water resistance as the hull is clear of the surface.

The *Connector* built in the 1850s was a novel idea. It was built in three sections joined by hinges, to help it ride over the waves more easily.

# Can we reach the planets?

In 1977, *Voyager I and II*, were launched into space. They are still travelling now, and by the end of this century will have left our solar system. In addition to scientific equipment, they are carrying long-playing records with greetings, sound effects and music from Earth. The length of time it takes to reach beyond our nearest neighbours in the universe makes the possibility of manned flights to outer planets very remote. Until a new source of propulsion is developed, we must be content with these robot explorers.

The Voyager space probes and the Viking Lander were launched from a Titan III-E Centaur rocket. This is the most powerful rocket outside the Soviet Union, since the Saturn V, which put man on the Moon.

*Voyager I* passing Saturn in about November 1980. The famous rings of this planet are not solid, as they appear, but composed mainly of ice and rock particles.

Lander released

Entering atmosphere

Parachute opens

Retro rockets

Lander unfolds

In June 1977, *Viking I* set off for Mars. It took almost a year to make the 708 million kms journey. On reaching Mars' orbit the lander was ejected and parachuted to the Martian surface. Twenty-five seconds after landing, its TV cameras sent the first pictures of the surface of Mars back to Earth. It not only photographed the surface, but also collected and analysed dust samples in an unsuccessful search for life.

# What are the transport giants?

Imagine a ship with a deck area big enough for four full-sized football pitches, and from keel to bridge a height equal to that of a twenty story building.

Not all the giants of the transport world are ships, although the current largest supertanker is the biggest moving object on Earth. The early era of aviation produced some giants in the past, the largest being the *Graf Zeppelin* airship at 245m long, and the Hughes Hercules flying boat with a wing span of 97.51 m.

In many cases, the reason for giants is economy, as a hugh supertanker is cheaper to run than two smaller vessels. Other reasons may be the size of the load the vehicle carries, as with the Saturn V rocket where almost the entire weight is its own fuel.

Some of the giants of the world of transport. They are all drawn to the same scale, so you can see how they compare.

Lockheed C5A Galaxy 75m

Articulated bus 23.16m

Articulated truck and trailer 41.14m

Russian Typhoon class submarine 180m

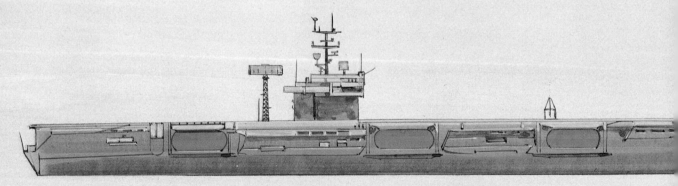

U.S.S. *Nimitz* aircraft carrier 332.84m

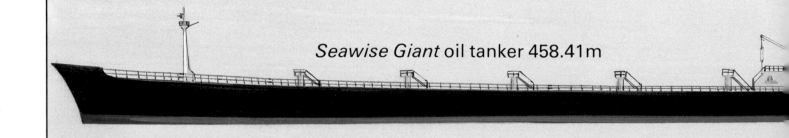

*Seawise Giant* oil tanker 458.41m

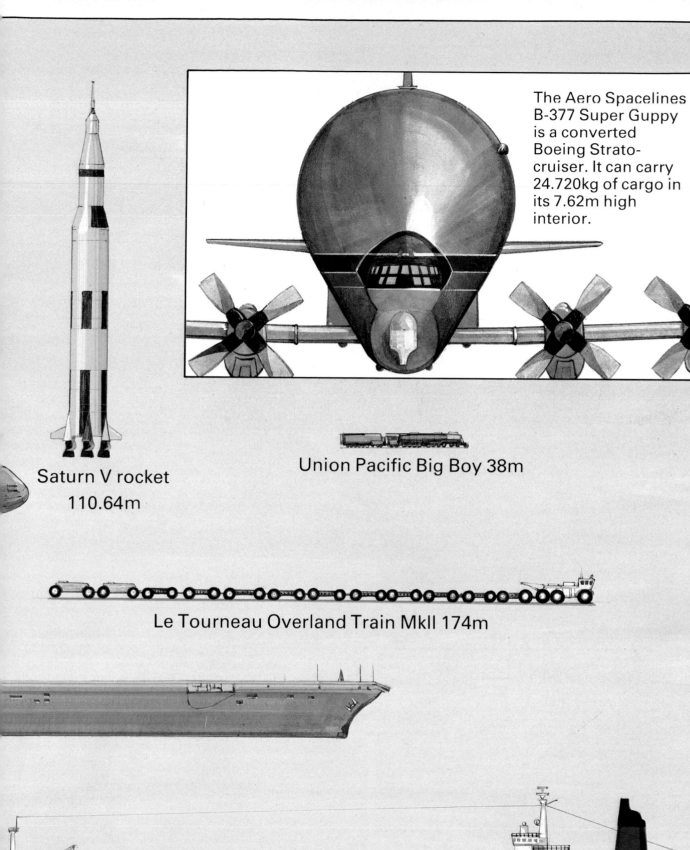

The Aero Spacelines B-377 Super Guppy is a converted Boeing Stratocruiser. It can carry 24.720kg of cargo in its 7.62m high interior.

Saturn V rocket 110.64m

Union Pacific Big Boy 38m

Le Tourneau Overland Train MkII 174m

# Can an aircraft ski-jump?

Although a helicopter can take-off and land vertically, it lacks the speed of a conventional aircraft.

Towards the end of World War II, the turbo-jet engine was introduced, but it was too late to have any real effect on the war. Even these early jet engines produced a thrust geater than their own weight. In 1947 the Rolls-Royce Nene turbojet came into service. This engine produced a thrust of four times its own weight. Using these engines, Rolls-Royce built a strange test aircraft, called the Flying Bedstead which proved the possibility of jet powered VTOL (Vertical Take-Off and Landing).

Since then, many different VTOL aircraft have been built, using both jets and propellers, for military as well as civil purposes.

The Rolls-Royce Flying Bedstead first flew in 1953. The lift was provided by two Nene turbojets, and the fine control for hovering by four swivelling, downward-facing nozzles.

The Bell X-22A was another solution to the problem of vertical flight. It was powered by large propellers in rotating tubes. In 1966 the test flights were a success, but it never went into production.

The Harrier, seen here in its naval role, is an extremely successful VTOL. The thrust of its jet engines is vectored, or channelled, through rotating nozzles on either side of the fuselage. In addition to its VTOL capacity, it can take off from an aircraft carrier, using a short ramp called a ski-jump.

The Ling-Temco-Vought XC-142A was another VTOL which was successfully tested, but never went into production. Designed as a military transport aircraft, it achieved vertical flight by rotating the entire wing.

# Which vehicles save lives?

Fire engines, ambulances, lifeboats and rescue helicopters are all vehicles designed to save lives. As technology advances, the problems of providing rescue services become more difficult.

In the early days of firefighting, a horse-drawn pump could supply the water for putting out fires, as most buildings were only two floors high. As buildings have increased in height, larger and more powerful vehicles are needed to carry long extending ladders and powerful pumps.

In these days of high-rise buildings, even the longest ladders and most powerful water pumps can only reach up a few storeys. The McDonnell Douglas SMS (Suspended Manoeuvring System) is designed for rescue services.

This huge articulated boom mounted on a vehicle, was known as a Cherry Picker. During a manned rocket test, it provided the astronaut's only means of escape.

The SMS pilot controls the vehicle by rotating the air nozzles. The SMS can move up to 45m in any direction from its position hanging from a helicopter.

The DSRV (Deep Submergence Rescue Vehicle) is small enough to be transported by air to a stricken submarine anywhere in the world.

# How deep can we go?

Man has always been fascinated by the ocean depths, but this mysterious world is as difficult to explore as outer space. The problem is not supplying oxygen to breathe, but protecting divers from the enormous pressure of the water. Even when diving a few metres below the surface, breathing becomes more difficult as the pressure increases. For a diver working in less than 50 metres, this pressure is not dangerous if he makes frequent stops to reduce the pressure gradually, on the way to the surface.

For a diver working deeper, this slow return to normal pressure, or decompression, can take a long time. After working for several hours at 300m the diver may need to stay in a steel decompression chamber for almost a week.

Protected in a strong steel vessel, we can go far deeper. *Trieste*, a bathyscaphe, meaning deep boat, went to a record depth of 10,917m in 1960, carrying a crew of two men into a world that had not been seen before.

The bathyscaphe *Trieste* made a historic voyage in 1960 – more than 10kms straight down into the deepest part of the Challenger Trench in the Pacific Ocean. The main part of *Trieste* is a huge tank filled with petrol, which is slowly replaced with sea water to make the vessel sink. The crew of two are in the tiny sphere beneath the craft, which is 2m in diameter and has steel walls 9cm thick.

The *Turtle* was, in fact, a military submarine propelled by winding handles connected to the screws. On the top of the vessel is a sharp drill, used to attach and explosive charge to an enemy ship.

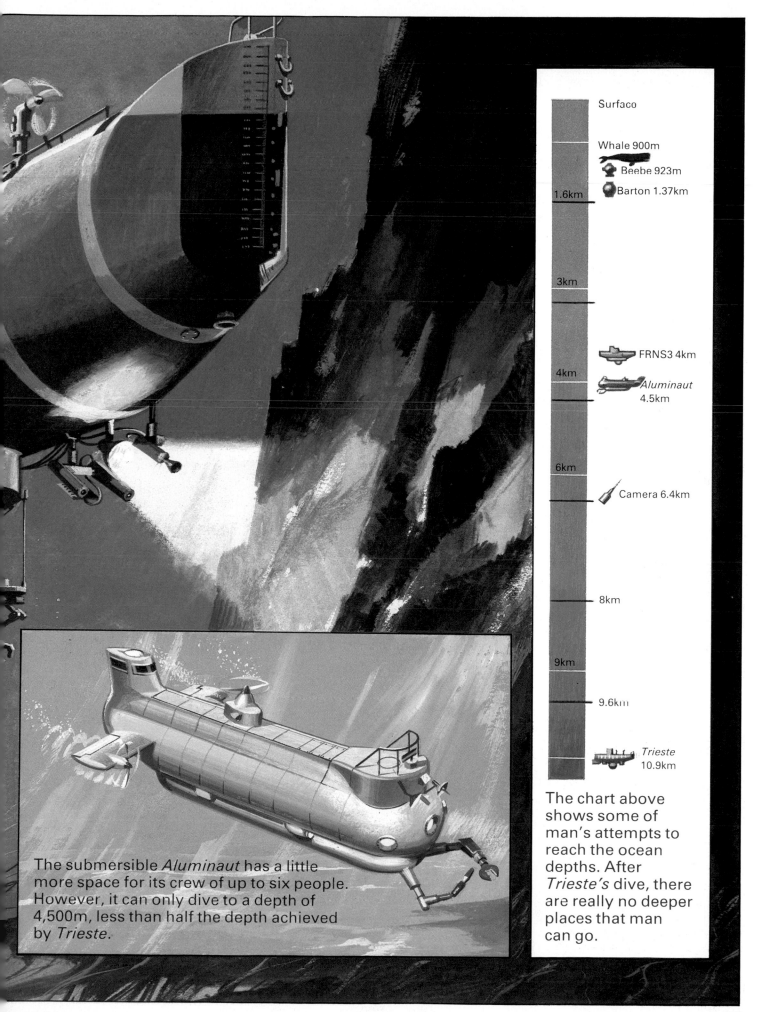

Surface

Whale 900m

Beebe 923m

Barton 1.37km

1.6km

3km

FRNS3 4km

4km

*Aluminaut* 4.5km

6km

Camera 6.4km

8km

9km

9.6km

*Trieste* 10.9km

The submersible *Aluminaut* has a little more space for its crew of up to six people. However, it can only dive to a depth of 4,500m, less than half the depth achieved by *Trieste*.

The chart above shows some of man's attempts to reach the ocean depths. After *Trieste's* dive, there are really no deeper places that man can go.

# What's an ATV?

ATVs (All Terrain Vehicles) are designed for all needs – exploration, warfare, sport, agriculture, anywhere without roads. Even space travel has produced an off-road vehicle – the Lunar Rover was used 386,000 km from the nearest road.

Probably the most common off-road vehicle is the Land Rover. These tough, four-wheel drive cars have been used in every corner of the world, from the Arctic and desert wastelands to the steamy tropical forests.

The earliest off-road vehicles were steam powered farm traction engines, shortly followed by the first tanks of World War 1. Since then vehicles have been built to cope with almost any type of terrain – sand, snow or swamp.

Not a joke, but a serious military test vehicle. The walking truck or Elephant as it is known, is a future possibility for transporting troops or supplies to places where even a tracked vehicle could not go.

The US Army's Twister is used for hauling supplies over rugged country. It is, in fact, two vehicles with separate bodies and engines, allowing it to climb a variety of obstacles with ease.

The Lunar Rover was carried by a Saturn V rocket on the *Apollo II* mission. It was used by the astronauts as a test vehicle to gather samples from a wider area.

This tractor is fitted with balloon floatation tyres, enabling it to travel on hard or soft ground, swamp, and even water.

Strictly a fun vehicle, the Sperry-Rand Tricart with its fat, soft tyres, can cope with sand, mud and rough ground.

# What's inside a Jumbo?

The success of the Boeing 747 Jumbo Jet is mainly due to its economic performance. A fully laden Jumbo uses only a gallon of fuel per passenger for 58.7km per passenger, which is about the same as a small family car. It has a maximum capacity of more than 500 passengers, and can reach a speed of 969kph.

This vast aircraft is 70.7m long, with a wingspan of 59.64m, and has been tested with a take-off weight of 386 tonnes.

The first Jumbo jet rolled out of the hangar on 30 September 1968. At that time, Boeing already had orders from 26 airlines, totalling 158 aircraft. The wide-bodied jet has advantages for passengers as well as airlines, and the standard of comfort in a 747 is a very long way from the wicker chairs and blankets of the early airliners operating in the 20s and 30s

The flight deck of the 747 showing the pilot's and co-pilot's controls. The training of pilots is a long and expensive process, much of it is now carried out by computer-controlled simulators.

A Boeing 747 Jumbo Jet cut away to show the interior. In this huge aircraft there is even a first-class lounge reached by a spiral staircase from the main deck.

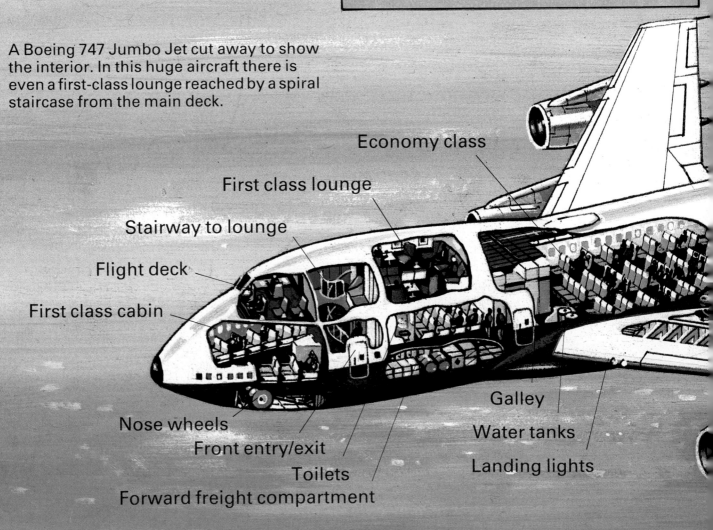

Economy class

First class lounge

Stairway to lounge

Flight deck

First class cabin

Nose wheels

Front entry/exit

Toilets

Forward freight compartment

Galley

Water tanks

Landing lights

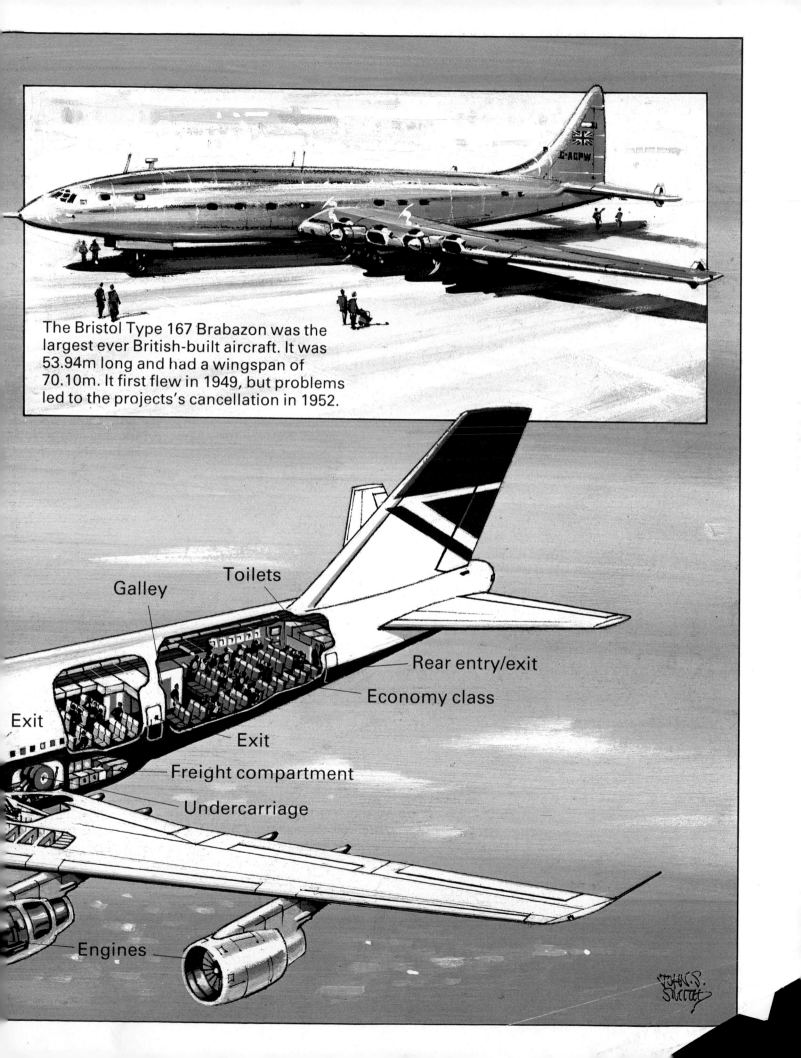

The Bristol Type 167 Brabazon was the largest ever British-built aircraft. It was 53.94m long and had a wingspan of 70.10m. It first flew in 1949, but problems led to the projects's cancellation in 1952.

Galley

Toilets

Rear entry/exit

Economy class

Exit

Exit

Freight compartment

Undercarriage

Engines

# How do you move mountains?

Man is rapidly changing the world around us —
building roads, dams, harbours and tunnels. In
order to carry out these constructions, many
millions of tonnes of earth and rock have to be
moved.

In the past, this was a long and difficult job,
needing thousands of workers and relying only
on human and animal muscle. Now the muscles
are mechanical and a machine can do, the
equivalent of a thousand men's work.

The size of earth-moving machines is difficult
to believe. Some built for opencast mining have
a boom as long as a football pitch, and a bucket
big enough to hold a house.

*Big Muskie*, a giant
walking dragline,
can carry 168cu.m of
soil and rock in its
scoop, enough to fill
18 railway goods
wagons.

The world's largest dump truck, the Terex Titan, has 3.5m diam. tyres.

The giant dragline excavators 'walk' on huge flat feet, which are lifted and moved forward by cams. These feet stop the vehicle from sinking into soft ground.

The Komatso underwater bulldozers can operate at depths of up to 60m. They are remotely controlled by the driver on land or in a boat. They are used for harbour construction, pipelaying and mining.

# Can you arrive before you leave?

If you board Concorde at London's Heathrow Airport at 12 noon on a flight to Kennedy Airport New York, you will arrive in time for lunch at 12 noon, in fact, you'll arrive even earlier! When the first prototype Concorde flew on 2 March 1969 a new age of supersonic air travel began. At a speed of 2156kph, twice the speed of sound, the journey to New York takes 3hrs 42mins. As the time difference between London and New York is 5hrs, you arrive 1hr 18 mins before you left.

Although Concorde is a success technically, it has not been a commercial success, most airlines preferring the slower, but more economical, Boeing 747 Jumbo Jet.

Concorde lands with the front of the aircraft held high. The nose is drooped 17° to allow the pilot a clear view of the runway ahead.

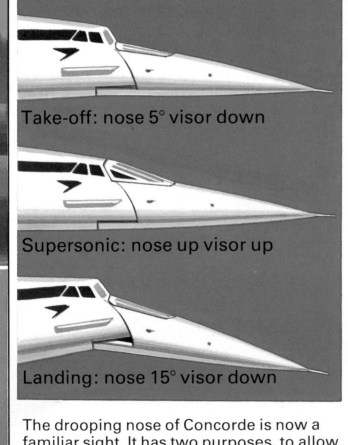

Take-off: nose 5° visor down

Supersonic: nose up visor up

Landing: nose 15° visor down

The drooping nose of Concorde is now a familiar sight. It has two purposes, to allow the pilot maximum visibility on landing, and to provide the minimum of air resistance in supersonic flight.

## INSIDE CONCORDE

- Flight deck
- Passenger cabins
- Rolls-Royce Olympus engines
- Undercarriage (retracted)
- Fuel tanks

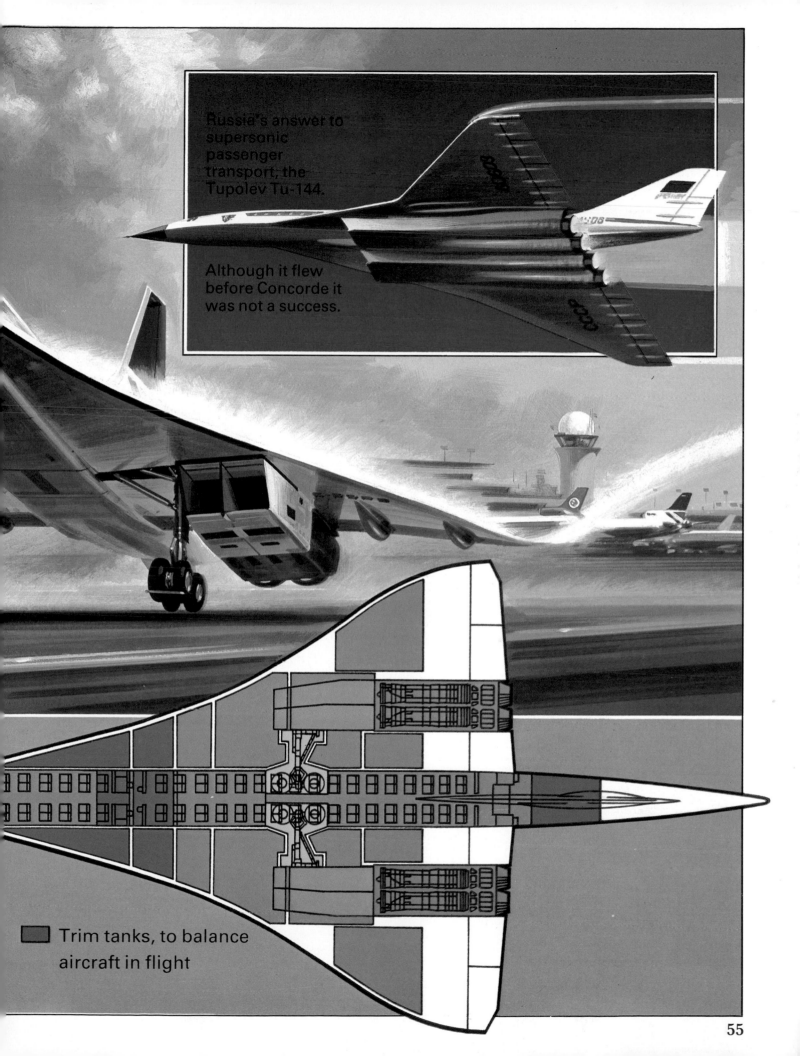

Russia's answer to
supersonic
passenger
transport, the
Tupolev Tu-144.

Although it flew
before Concorde it
was not a success.

Trim tanks, to balance
aircraft in flight

# How will the Shuttle be used?

At 7am on 12 April 1981, a major event in the history of space travel took place at NASA's Kennedy Space Center. The first re-usable spacecraft was launched, and the Space Shuttle programme became a reality.

Until that time, millions of dollars worth of space technology had either drifted round, orbiting the Earth, or burned up on re-entering the Earth's atmosphere. The Shuttle programme has great potential in reducing the cost of future projects, especially the launching of satellites into Earth orbit. It many also be used in the transport and construction of orbiting space stations. These could provide a permanent base for scientists, who would be replaced at regular intervals by a new team ferried from Earth in the Shuttle.

*Columbia,* the first Space Shuttle orbiter, lifts off from Kennedy Space Center, lifted from the ground by 3000 tonnes of thrust from the huge booster rockets.

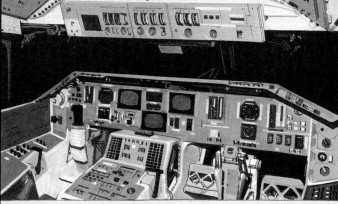

The Shuttle flight deck may look very complex but, in fact, it is little different from any modern jet. Most of the routine operations and systems checking are carried out by sophisticated computers.

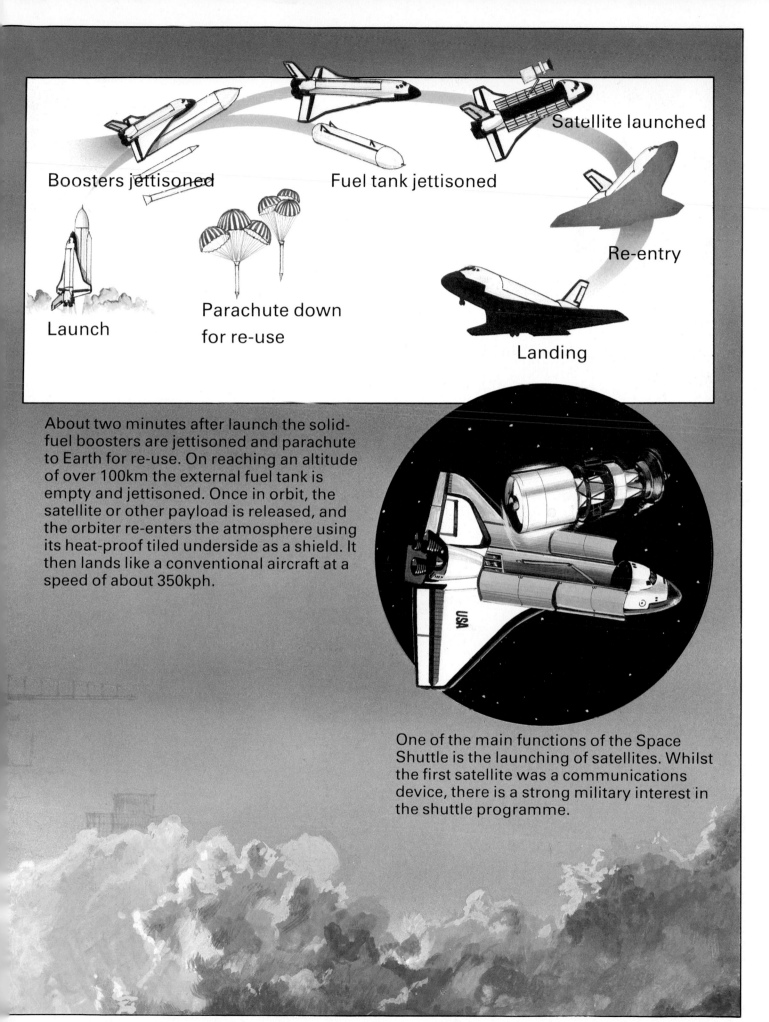

Satellite launched

Boosters jettisoned

Fuel tank jettisoned

Re-entry

Launch

Parachute down
for re-use

Landing

About two minutes after launch the solid-fuel boosters are jettisoned and parachute to Earth for re-use. On reaching an altitude of over 100km the external fuel tank is empty and jettisoned. Once in orbit, the satellite or other payload is released, and the orbiter re-enters the atmosphere using its heat-proof tiled underside as a shield. It then lands like a conventional aircraft at a speed of about 350kph.

One of the main functions of the Space Shuttle is the launching of satellites. Whilst the first satellite was a communications device, there is a strong military interest in the shuttle programme.

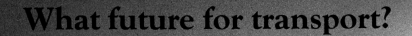

# What future for transport?

During the past fifty years transport has changed a great deal, but although these changes may appear to be dramatic, the basic means of mechanical transport have remained the same. Motorcars, aircraft, ships and trains are all still in use. In some cases, the power-source has changed from steam to electric or gas turbine, and from propellers to the jet engine. Very few entirely new means of transport have emerged, perhaps hovercraft, helicopters, vertical take-off aircraft and space craft, being the most important.

We could see a similar situation in fifty years time, with continuing improvement of our current means of transport, and possibly a few exciting new ideas. New technology may be applied to old ideas, and we could once again see airships as large as ocean liners in the sky.

An idea for speeding up the loading and unloading of the cargo ships of the future. The cargo compartments fit between the permanent bow and stern sections.

The Space Shuttle is the beginning of a new era in space travel. One day space-liners may carry passengers to other planets.